Editorial Project Manager
Erica N. Russikoff, M.A.

Editor in Chief
Brent L. Fox, M. Ed.

Creative Director
Sarah M. Fournier

Cover Artist
Diem Pascarella

Illustrator
Crystal-Dawn Keitz

Imaging
Amanda R. Harter

Publisher
Mary D. Smith, M.S. Ed.

CHANGE YOUR MINDSET

3–4

TCR 8310

Growth Mindset Activities for the Classroom

- Teaches, demonstrates, and reinforces a growth mindset
- Contains 12 comprehensive units, each one illustrating a different inspirational person and growth-mindset mantra
- Includes reading passages and individual, small-group, and whole-class practice that require short and long responses

Teacher Created Resources

Author
Samantha Chagollan

Teacher Created Resources
12621 Western Avenue
Garden Grove, CA 92841
www.teachercreated.com

ISBN: 978-1-4206-8310-3

©2020 Teacher Created Resources
Reprinted, 2021
Made in U.S.A.

Teacher Created Resources

TABLE OF CONTENTS

INTRODUCTION

In 1988, a group of researchers, including Stanford psychology professor Carol Dweck, studied students' responses to failure.

Some students rebounded well, while others were derailed by simple setbacks.

After extensive research with thousands of students, Dr. Dweck came up with the terms *fixed mindset* and *growth mindset* to encapsulate the differences between how all of us think about learning.

Simply put, having a growth mindset means you believe that you can and will improve with effort. A fixed mindset, by comparison, means that you believe you have a fixed amount of intelligence or talent that will never change.

We all have these two mindsets, but what Dr. Dweck has shown is that students are more likely to succeed once they take on a growth mindset and understand that they can get better at anything with time and effort.

In a fixed mindset, challenges are avoided, criticism is ignored, and students feel threatened by the success of others and are quick to give up when things get hard.

In a growth mindset, mistakes are seen as learning opportunities, challenges are welcomed, and students persevere with effort, leading to a desire to learn even more.

Teaching students about a growth mindset and the science behind it, including brain plasticity, has helped countless students to grasp the idea that they can achieve their dreams, no matter their starting points.

The activities in this book support the growth-mindset philosophy. With practice and positive reinforcement, students will be able to adopt this flexible, supportive, and uplifting perspective.

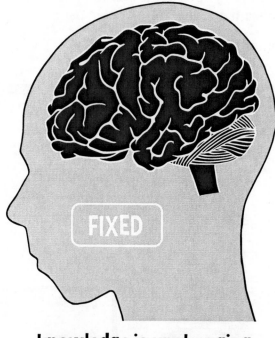

knowledge is unchanging

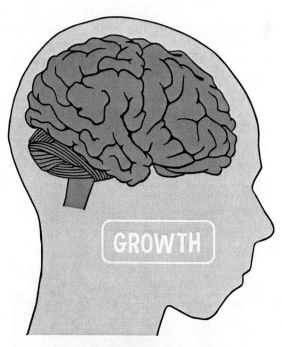

knowledge can grow

HOW TO USE THIS BOOK

For practical application in the classroom, this book provides 12 units that are each focused on one of the following growth-mindset mantras:

- ★ I will do my best.
- ★ I can put in more time and effort.
- ★ I can learn from my mistakes.
- ★ I believe I can do it.
- ★ I can reach my goals.
- ★ I am not afraid of difficult tasks.

- ★ I can come up with creative solutions.
- ★ I can improve with practice.
- ★ I value thoughtful feedback.
- ★ I am capable of learning new things.
- ★ I can keep going when things are tough.
- ★ I can train my brain.

Each unit includes an overview for the teacher and six student activities to support each mantra.

Reading Passage: To help students understand the meaning of the mantra, each unit includes a nonfiction narrative that features the story of someone who exemplifies that mantra.

Short-Answer Activity: After reading, students are asked a handful of questions that will check for understanding and provide potential talking points for a larger class discussion about the mantra.

Small-Group Activity: Students are asked to gather in small groups and collaborate to gain a deeper understanding.

Whole-Class Activity: The class is asked to reflect on their learning together; whole-class activities provide a perfect forum for learning about growth-mindset principles and practices, too.

Journal Prompt: Students are given the opportunity to reflect on what they have learned in the unit.

Growing Beyond: An extension activity is presented to take learning beyond the classroom for deeper understanding. *Note:* This activity is listed on the lesson plan and does not have its own page.

All the activities in this book have been aligned to the Common Core State Standards (CCSS). A correlations chart is included on pages 79–80.

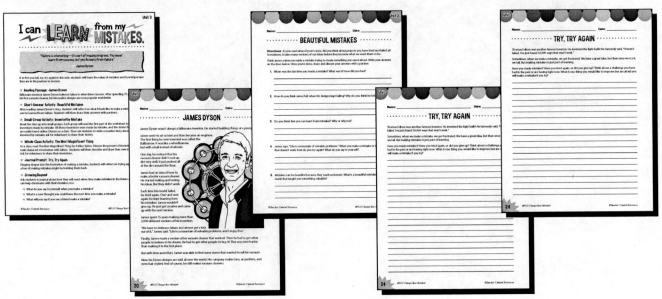

TEACHER SELF-ASSESSMENT

Before you dive into teaching growth mindset, it's a good idea to know where you stand.

Read each statement and note whether this is something you always, sometimes, or never do or say. On a separate piece of paper, take notes that might be helpful for your own self-reflection.

	Always	Sometimes	Never
1. I am inspired when others around me succeed.	☐	☐	☐
2. I believe that intelligence can improve.	☐	☐	☐
3. I learn from my mistakes.	☐	☐	☐
4. When things get challenging, I am likely to give up.	☐	☐	☐
5. If something doesn't work, I try a different strategy.	☐	☐	☐
6. I receive feedback and criticism well.	☐	☐	☐
7. There are some things I am just not good at.	☐	☐	☐
8. I set goals and monitor my progress.	☐	☐	☐
9. I have a set way of doing things that works for me.	☐	☐	☐
10. Some students just aren't good at certain things.	☐	☐	☐
11. I love to learn new things.	☐	☐	☐
12. I notice when I am thinking negative thoughts, and I am able to change those thoughts to more encouraging ones.	☐	☐	☐

We all fluctuate between both fixed and growth mindsets, but it's important to know for yourself which side you favor.

In this assessment, items 4, 7, 9, and 10 are fixed-mindset statements. The rest are growth-mindset statements.

Each mantra featured in this book is a growth-mindset statement that you can reinforce in your classroom. The more you use and model these mantras for your students, the greater their understanding of the growth mindset will be.

PARENT LETTER

As you're teaching your students about growth mindset, bring parents into the picture so this attitude can be practiced at home, too.

Consider creating a parent letter that explains what the growth mindset is, and how parents can support their child's learning. Here's an example:

Dear Parents,

Many of us grew up believing that either we were smart or we weren't. We were either good at something or we weren't.

But now, through scientific research, we know that simply isn't true. Our brains can grow and change, and when students are aware of this, they can get inspired to learn more.

I'm working with your child to help develop a "growth mindset." Someone with a growth mindset gives their best effort, learns from mistakes, and finds creative solutions to problems.

I would love for you to help support this growth mindset at home, too. Here are some ideas for how you can help:

★ Remind your child that mistakes are okay. We all make them! Each time we try and fail, our brains get stronger, and this is how we learn to persevere when things get tough.

★ Praise effort over achievement. It's the process that counts, so compliment your child for the work they put in, the creativity they displayed, or the determination they showed.

★ Ask questions like, "How were you challenged today? What mistakes did you make? What did you learn?"

★ Help your child practice growth-mindset self-talk. If you hear your child say something like, "I can't do this!" have them try saying, "I can't do this yet, but I'll keep trying."

The more you can talk about this and model it for your child, the more they will understand that intelligence can change and achievement is never out of reach when effort is given.

Thank you for your support!

I will DO MY BEST.

> "We all have dreams. But in order to make dreams come into reality, it takes an awful lot of determination, dedication, self-discipline, and effort."
>
> ~ Jesse Owens

Focusing students on what it means to give your best effort to a challenge will help them learn that great things can be achieved with effort.

★ Reading Passage: Jesse Owens

One of the most famous athletes in history, Jesse Owens had a dedication to excellence that resulted in new world records and Olympic gold.

★ Short-Answer Activity: Doing Your Best

After reading about Jesse Owens, students will reflect on what it means to do your best.

★ Small-Group Activity: The Best of Me

Using a graphic organizer, students will work in small groups to complete a worksheet about themselves and share it with their groups.

★ Whole-Class Activity: The Effort-ometer

As a class, students will create a class poster that is a visual reminder of how much effort is being used at any given time.

★ Journal Prompt: Your Best

To create a deeper connection with how it feels to do your best, students will journal about a time when they were proud of doing their best; volunteers can share their answers with the class.

★ Growing Beyond

Talk to students about the Olympic Games and what it means to win a gold, silver, or bronze medal. Let them know that sometimes, even when they give their best effort, they don't take home a medal. Discuss as a class what it means to "go for the gold"—to give your very best, no matter what the outcome may be. Remind students that when they put forth their best efforts, they can always be proud of what they achieve, whether they take home a medal or not.

Ask students to write and draw pictures of their answers to the following question: How will I go for the gold in the future?

Name: _____   Date: _____

JESSE OWENS

Jesse Owens is one of the most famous athletes in history. He was a track and field star who won gold medals and set world records.

But Jesse wasn't always so strong. As a child, Jesse was sometimes so sick he had to stay in bed all day.

Jesse was the youngest of 10 children. Along with his brothers and sisters, Jesse was expected to work and pick cotton to help his family.

But whenever he could, Jesse loved to play and run in the fields.

"I always loved running," he said. "I wasn't very good at it, but I loved it because it was something you could do all by yourself.

"You could go in any direction, fast or slow as you wanted, fighting the wind if you felt like it, seeking out new sights just on the strength of your feet and the courage of your lungs."

By the time Jesse was in fifth grade, he had grown stronger. He was asked to join the track team at school. Soon, he set a new record for the 100-yard dash.

Jesse kept running and competing, and soon he went to college. He studied and practiced for his track meets. And he worked three jobs to pay for school.

Jesse never stopped giving his best to reach his dreams. Soon, he was setting new world records. He even joined the Olympic Team and won four gold medals in 1936.

Name: _____   **Date:** _____

· · · · · · · · · · · DOING YOUR BEST · · · · · · · · · ·

Directions: In a small group, discuss these questions:

★ What does it mean to do your best?

★ How does it feel when you do your best?

★ What might stop you from doing your best?

Directions: On your own, answer the questions on the lines below.

1. Jesse loved to run even though he wasn't very good at it at first. Is there something you love to do that isn't easy? Write about it.

   _____

   _____

   _____

2. What are some adjectives you would use to describe Jesse Owens?

   _____

   _____

3. Would you use any of those adjectives to describe yourself? List which ones and explain why they apply to you.

   _____

   _____

   _____

4. Why is it important to give your best effort?

   _____

   _____

   _____

5. Who or what motivates you to do your best?

   _____

   _____

   _____

Name: _____ **Date:** _____

· · · · · · · · · · · · THE BEST OF ME · · · · · · · · · ·

Directions: Complete this graphic organizer, filling out what you think is the "best" of you. You can write your answers and draw pictures. Just like Jesse Owens, you may have hobbies or skills that you love to do even if they are hard sometimes. Add these ideas below. Then, in a group with two to three other students, share your answers.

The Best of

_____
(name)

★ My Best Qualities ★

★ Words My Friends Use to Describe Me ★

★ My Favorite Activity ★

★ My Superpower ★

#8310 Change Your Mindset   ©*Teacher Created Resources*

Name: _____ **Date:** _____

THE EFFORT-OMETER

Directions: As a class, create "The Effort-ometer"—a poster-sized thermometer that "measures" the level of effort you or other students offer at any given time. This graphic representation will help remind everyone that greater effort can result in greater results.

1. Begin with a large piece of posterboard or butcher paper.

2. Draw the outline of a mercury thermometer, with a bulb at the bottom and lines to represent measures up to the top.

3. Starting at the bottom, color the first section and label it "No Effort: I didn't try at all." Pause and discuss this statement with your classmates. Can you remember a time when you didn't give any effort? What did that feel like?

4. Move on to the next label: "Tiny Effort: I tried, but I didn't finish."

5. Continue up the Effort-ometer with these labels, adding any others you feel are appropriate:

   ★ "Small Effort: I finished, but I rushed."

   ★ "Okay Effort: I did it, but there is more I could have done."

   ★ "Good Effort: I could do more next time!"

   ★ "Great Effort: There's one more thing I could do."

   ★ "Awesome Effort: I did my very best!"

6. Add color so each section gets darker, as it gets nearer to the top—where effort is the greatest.

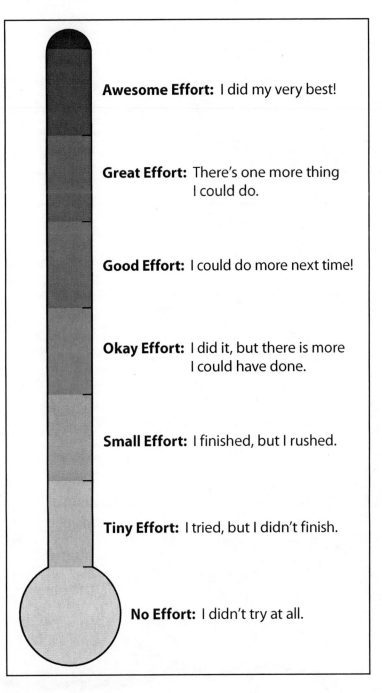

Awesome Effort: I did my very best!

Great Effort: There's one more thing I could do.

Good Effort: I could do more next time!

Okay Effort: I did it, but there is more I could have done.

Small Effort: I finished, but I rushed.

Tiny Effort: I tried, but I didn't finish.

No Effort: I didn't try at all.

Name: _____   **Date:** _____

· · · · · · · · · · · · · · YOUR BEST · · · · · · · · · · · ·

Think of a time when you were proud of yourself. Were you doing your best? How did it feel to do your best? Write about it on the lines. Then draw a picture in the box to show what it felt like to do your best.

_____

_____

_____

_____

_____

_____

_____

_____

_____

_____

I can PUT IN MORE TIME and EFFORT.

> "I always wanted to be someone better the next day than I was the day before."
>
> Sidney Poitier

Achievements require dedication and perseverance. In this unit, students will learn the value of putting in time and effort to achieve their goals.

★ Reading Passage: Sidney Poitier

For Sidney Poitier, acting didn't come easy. But after careful study and effort, he became an Oscar-winning actor.

★ Short-Answer Activity: Time & Effort

Reflecting on Sidney Poitier's story, students will answer questions about the narrative and then pair up to share their answers.

★ Small-Group Activity: How Much Effort Do I Give?

Students will take a short self-reflective quiz with growth-mindset statements and then break into small groups to discuss their answers. Encourage students to reflect on one another's answers, to reinforce growth mindset in all students.

★ Whole-Class Activity: 10,000 Hours

Exploring the popular idea that it takes 10,000 hours to master anything, the class will discuss and make a poster together of skills they might like to master.

★ Journal Prompt: Practice Makes Progress

Students will reflect on their dreams for the future and where they might like to spend more time and effort.

★ Growing Beyond

Once students have identified skills they would like to practice, ask them to reflect on how they will take small steps toward mastery. Ask them to write their answers to these questions individually, and then discuss as a class so that students may inspire one another.

- ★ What is the skill you want to practice more?
- ★ Why do you want to improve this skill?
- ★ When will you set aside time to practice this skill?
- ★ How will you practice?
- ★ Who do you know that is already good at this skill and could help you?

Name: _____   Date: _____

SIDNEY POITIER

Sidney Poitier was the first African American to win an Academy Award for best actor. But when he was first starting out, that dream seemed nearly impossible.

Sidney's parents were from the Bahamian islands. Sidney was born two months early, while his parents were on vacation in Miami. The family moved back to the Bahamas when Sidney was still a baby.

Sidney's father was a tomato farmer on Cat Island. The family worked hard, but they were very poor. When the farm failed, the family moved to another island, Nassau.

As a young boy, Sidney seemed to get into trouble a lot. His father sent him to live with an uncle in Miami when Sidney was 15. When he was 16, Sidney decided to move to New York City.

It was there that he fell in love with acting. He was excited to try out for a local theater. But at his audition, he messed up his lines. They said his accent was too thick. The director told him, "Stop wasting your time. Get a job as a dishwasher!"

But those harsh words didn't stop Sidney. Instead of making him want to give up, they made him work harder. He knew he had to put in time and effort to achieve his dreams.

Sidney started to study the TV news. He listened to the way the reporters spoke. He practiced speaking like them to change his accent. To pay for acting lessons, Sidney worked as a janitor at the theater.

Finally, his hard work paid off. He got his first role in a play. And that was just the start!

Sidney Poitier went on to star in and direct more than 30 movies. In 1963, he made film history when he won an Academy Award for his role in *Lilies of the Field*. He has received many other awards since then, including the Presidential Medal of Freedom.

Name: _____ **Date:** _____

TIME & EFFORT

Directions: Think about Sidney Poitier's story. Then write your answers to the questions below. When you're finished, share your answers with a partner.

1. How do you think Sidney felt when he was told his accent was too strong? Why do you think he felt that way?

   _____

   _____

   _____

2. Sidney didn't let the director's words discourage him. He was *determined* to work toward his dreams. Write down some other adjectives to describe Sidney.

   _____

   _____

   _____

3. Do you think it was hard for Sidney to keep studying acting, even when others told him he wasn't very good at it? What do you think kept him going?

   _____

   _____

   _____

4. Sidney kept putting in more time and effort to become good at acting. Why do you think that was important?

   _____

   _____

   _____

5. How do you think Sidney felt when he won his Academy Award? Why do you think this?

   _____

   _____

   _____

Name: _____   Date: _____

· · · · · · · **HOW MUCH EFFORT DO I GIVE?** · · · · · · ·

Directions: Take this quiz to see what is true for you. Read each statement and place an **X** in the box that matches your answer. When you're done, form a group with two to three other students and discuss your answers. Give your group members feedback on their responses so you can help one another improve!

	Always True	Sometimes True	Rarely True
1. I don't give up easily.	☐	☐	☐
2. If something is hard, I keep trying.	☐	☐	☐
3. I like to try new things.	☐	☐	☐
4. When I'm not good at something, I give more effort.	☐	☐	☐
5. I can cheer myself up.	☐	☐	☐
6. I give my best effort.	☐	☐	☐
7. I make mistakes, but I learn from them.	☐	☐	☐
8. I like to take on new challenges.	☐	☐	☐
9. I try to improve.	☐	☐	☐
10. I love to learn!	☐	☐	☐
11. I try things I am not very good at.	☐	☐	☐
12. When I see a friend struggling, I try to help.	☐	☐	☐
13. I choose my attitude.	☐	☐	☐
14. I take my time.	☐	☐	☐
15. I'm ready for the next challenge!	☐	☐	☐

Name: _____   Date: _____

10,000 HOURS

Directions: Have you ever heard that it takes 10,000 hours to become an expert at anything? Some people think it's true, and others don't. Either way, we know it takes a lot of time and effort to master a skill.

As a class, we're going to make a list of the skills we might like to master someday.

Begin with a large piece of poster board or butcher paper. At the top, write "Becoming Experts."

What do you want to become an expert at? Here are some ideas:

★ Playing a musical instrument

★ Baking a cake

★ Learning the constellations

★ Painting a picture

★ Playing soccer

★ Helping sick people by discovering cures

★ Doing karate (Goal: black belt!)

★ Writing short stories

On the poster board or butcher paper, list all the skills your class wants to master. Keep it up in the classroom so everyone can see it!

Name: _____   **Date:** _____

· · · · · · · · PRACTICE MAKES PROGRESS · · · · · · · ·

Musician Ed Sheeran said, "When people say, 'You are so talented and you're born with natural talent,' I say, 'No.' You have to really learn and practice."

Like Ed Sheeran, Sidney Poitier had a dream of becoming a successful artist. But he had to put a lot of time and effort in to make his dream come true.

What is something you would like to put more time and effort toward? Who or what do you dream of becoming? What kind of effort do you think you will need to put in to make it happen? Answer these questions on the lines below.

_____

_____

_____

_____

_____

_____

_____

_____

_____

_____

_____

_____

_____

_____

_____

_____

_____

_____

_____

_____

I can LEARN from my MISTAKES.

> "Failure is interesting—it's part of making progress. You never learn from success, but you do learn from failure."
>
> ~ James Dyson

If at first you fail, try, try again! In this unit, students will learn the value of mistakes and how important they are in the journey to success.

★ Reading Passage: James Dyson

Billionaire inventor James Dyson believes failure is what drives success. After spending 15 years creating his first vacuum cleaner, his innovative designs are now popular worldwide.

★ Short-Answer Activity: Beautiful Mistakes

After reading James Dyson's story, students will reflect on what it feels like to make a mistake and what can be learned from failure. Students will then share their answers with partners.

★ Small-Group Activity: Invented by Mistake

Break the class up into small groups. Each group will read the first part of the worksheet together, about inventions made by mistake. All these inventions were made by mistake, and the stories behind each are easily found online. Discuss as a class. Then ask students to write a creative story about something invented by mistake; ask for volunteers to share their stories.

★ Whole-Class Activity: The Most Magnificent Thing

As a class, read *The Most Magnificent Thing* by Ashley Spires. Discuss the process of inventing and the main character's frustration with failure. Students will then describe and draw their own inventions. Ask for volunteers to share their inventions.

★ Journal Prompt: Try, Try Again

Digging deeper into the frustration of making a mistake, students will reflect on trying again and how a fear of making mistakes might be holding them back.

★ Growing Beyond

Ask students to journal about how they will react when they make mistakes in the future and how they can help classmates with their mistakes, too.

- ★ What do you say to yourself when you make a mistake?
- ★ What is a new thought you could have the next time you make a mistake?
- ★ What will you say if you see a friend make a mistake?

Name: _____   **Date:** _____

JAMES DYSON

James Dyson wasn't always a billionaire inventor. He started building things at a young age.

James went to art school and then became an engineer. The first thing he ever invented was called the Ballbarrow. It was like a wheelbarrow, but with a ball instead of wheels.

One day, he noticed that his vacuum cleaner didn't suck up dirt very well. It just pushed all of the dirt around the floor.

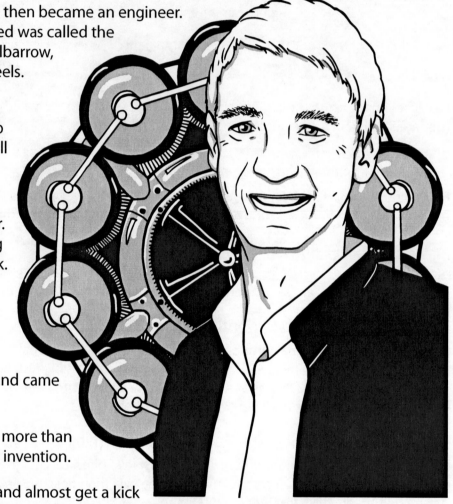

James had an idea of how to make a better vacuum cleaner. He started making and testing his ideas. But they didn't work.

Each time his model failed, he tried again. Over and over again, he kept learning from his mistakes. James wouldn't give up. He just got creative and came up with the next version.

James spent 15 years making more than 5,000 different versions of his invention.

"We have to embrace failure and almost get a kick out of it," James said. "Life is a mountain of solvable problems, and I enjoy that."

Finally, James made a version of his vacuum cleaner that worked. Then he had to get other people to believe in his dream. He had to get other people to buy it! That was even harder than making it in the first place.

But with time and effort, James was able to find some stores that wanted to sell his vacuum.

Now, his Dyson designs are sold all over the world. His company makes fans, air purifiers, and even hair stylers! And of course, he still makes vacuum cleaners.

Name: _____   **Date:** _____

· · · · · · · · · · BEAUTIFUL MISTAKES · · · · · · · · · ·

Directions: As you read James Dyson's story, did you think about projects you have tried and failed at? Sometimes, it takes many versions of our ideas before they become what we want them to be.

Think about a time you made a mistake trying to create something you cared about. Write your answers on the lines below. Once you're done, share and discuss your answers with a partner.

1. When was the last time you made a mistake? What was it? How did you feel?

   _____
   _____
   _____

2. How do you think James felt when his designs kept failing? Why do you think he felt that way?

   _____
   _____
   _____

3. Do you think that you can learn from mistakes? Why or why not?

   _____
   _____
   _____

4. James says, "Life is a mountain of solvable problems." When you make a mistake or try something that doesn't work, how do you try again? What do you say to yourself?

   _____
   _____
   _____

5. Mistakes can be beautiful because they teach us lessons. What is a beautiful mistake you have made that taught you something valuable?

   _____
   _____
   _____

Name: _____ **Date:** _____

· · · · · · · · · · INVENTED BY MISTAKE · · · · · · · · · ·

Directions: In a group with two to three other students, find out which of these things was invented by mistake. Circle your answers. Then as a class, discuss your choices.

potato chips   microwave oven   Post-it Notes

Silly Putty   fireworks   chocolate chip cookies

Directions: On your own, write a creative story about an invention that was made by mistake. If you need more room, use a separate piece of paper. Here are some questions to get you started:

⭐ Who invented it?

⭐ What were they trying to invent?

⭐ How many mistakes did they make?

⭐ What did they end up inventing instead?

⭐ How does their new invention make the world a better place?

_____

_____

_____

_____

_____

_____

_____

_____

_____

_____

_____

_____

_____

_____

_____

Name: _____ **Date:** _____

· · · · · · · THE MOST MAGNIFICENT THING · · · · · ·

Directions: Create your own Magnificent Thing! Answer these questions, and then draw your invention below.

1. What is your invention idea?

   _____

   _____

2. What problem does it solve?

   _____

   _____

3. How does it work?

   _____

   _____

4. What is it called?

   _____

My Invention

Name: _____ **Date:** _____

TRY, TRY AGAIN

Thomas Edison was another famous inventor. He invented the light bulb! He famously said, "I haven't failed. I've just found 10,000 ways that won't work."

Sometimes, when we make a mistake, we get frustrated. We have a great idea, but then once we try it, we fail. But making mistakes is just part of learning.

Have you made mistakes? Have you tried again, or did you give up? Think about a challenge you have had in the past or are having right now. What is one thing you would like to improve but are afraid you will make a mistake if you try?

_____

_____

_____

_____

_____

_____

_____

_____

_____

_____

_____

_____

_____

_____

_____

_____

_____

_____

_____

I BELIEVE I can DO IT.

> "The big secret in life is that there is no big secret. Whatever your goal, you can get there if you're willing to work."
>
> ~ Oprah Winfrey

Believing in yourself is key to continued learning and emotional development. As students build confidence, they are more willing to take on greater challenges and grow.

★ Reading Passage: Oprah Winfrey

The world knows Oprah Winfrey as a powerful woman, but it took a lot of confidence to get there. Students will learn how believing in yourself, in spite of rejection, can lead to success.

★ Short-Answer Activity: Confidence Is Key

Students will pair up, look up the definition of the word *confidence*, and analyze a quote from the reading. Then they will independently answer questions about the narrative. Consider discussing as a class afterward, and have students share what they learned with one another.

★ Small-Group Activity: Say Something Nice

To build confidence, students will practice complimenting one another in small groups and then give compliments to themselves as well. These can be used as future reminders and confidence boosters.

★ Whole-Class Activity: Expert Advice

Students will pair up and interview each other about an area of expertise, giving each other advice on how to become an expert, too. Students will then draw pictures of their partners being experts. Once the interviews are complete, student pairs will share their responses by introducing themselves and explaining their expertise to the class.

★ Journal Prompt: Believe It, Be It

Reflecting back on how it feels to believe in themselves, students will journal about confidence and who they are becoming.

★ Growing Beyond

Thinking about what they have learned about belief and confidence, students will draw self-portraits. Then they will write statements around the outside that begin with "I am…" and are focused on positive traits to continue building self-confidence and reinforce the growth mindset.

Examples include "I am a good friend," "I am kind," "I am a good listener," and "I am confident." These statements can also be printed and cut out ahead of time so students can make collages around their portraits.

Name: _____   Date: _____

OPRAH WINFREY

You may know Oprah Winfrey as a famous journalist and wealthy woman. But long before she became the star she is now, Oprah lived a very different life.

When she was a little girl, Oprah was poor and so unhappy that she ran away from home. As she grew up, she studied hard in school and went to college. She always believed in herself, even when it seemed as though no one else did.

After she graduated, she got her first job at a TV station in Nashville. Then she was offered an even better job in Baltimore. She became the co-anchor of the news.

After just seven months, her producer told her she was "unfit for television news." She lost her job.

But she didn't lose her hope. Oprah loved working in television, and she wasn't ready to give up yet. She loved telling other people's stories and wanted to keep doing just that.

Even though other people may have doubted her talent, she never did. She believed in herself, and she believed in her dreams.

Oprah said, "Be the one thing you think you cannot do. Fail at it. Try again. Do better the second time. The only people who never tumble are those who never mount the high wire. This is your moment, own it."

Soon she was offered another job on a new show called *People Are Talking*. It was a daytime talk show, and it became a hit.

She went on to host *The Oprah Winfrey Show* for 25 seasons. Oprah is now known all over the world and is one of the world's wealthiest people.

She never gave up on her dreams, and now she helps others achieve their dreams, too. Oprah opened a school for girls in South Africa in 2007 called the Oprah Winfrey Leadership Academy. The school has almost 300 students who Oprah hopes will become future leaders.

Name: _____   Date: _____

CONFIDENCE IS KEY

Directions: Find a partner. Think about what you read about Oprah Winfrey. Then discuss the following questions together:

★ Oprah said this about failing: "The only people who never tumble are those who never mount the high wire." What do you think that means?

★ Look up the word *confidence* in the dictionary. Do you think Oprah has confidence?

Directions: On your own, answer the questions on the lines below.

1. How do you think Oprah Winfrey felt when her producer said she was "unfit for television news"?

_____

_____

_____

_____

2. What do you think would have happened if Oprah had given up after she lost her job?

_____

_____

_____

_____

3. What is one quality you would say Oprah has? Do you have the same quality? Explain your answer.

_____

_____

_____

_____

4. What is one question you would ask Oprah about her success if you could?

_____

_____

_____

_____

Name: _____ **Date:** _____

SAY SOMETHING NICE

Directions: Form a group with two other students. Sit in a circle. One at a time, turn to the person on your right and give them a compliment. When you get a compliment, write it in the first box below. Write the name of the person who gave you the compliment, too.

Then go back around the circle the other way. Turn to the person on your left and give them a compliment. Write the compliment in the second box below.

Now, it's your turn. Write at least three more compliments to yourself on the list below.

Thanks for the compliment, _____!

Thanks for the compliment, _____!

Compliments to myself:

1. _____

_____

_____

2. _____

_____

_____

3. _____

_____

_____

#8310 Change Your Mindset ©*Teacher Created Resources*

Name: _____   **Date:** _____

• • • • • • • • • • • • • EXPERT ADVICE • • • • • • • • • • • •

Directions: Find a partner. Take turns asking each other the following questions. Record your partner's answers below, and finish by drawing a picture of your partner being an expert. Share your answers and drawing with your class.

1. What is one thing you are really good at?

   _____

   _____

2. How did you get so good at it?

   _____

   _____

   _____

3. What kind of advice would you give me if I wanted to be really good at that, too?

   _____

   _____

   _____

_____ is an expert at _____.
　(your partner's name)　　　　　　　　　　　　　　　(what they are good at)

Name: _____ **Date:** _____

BELIEVE IT, BE IT

Have you ever said to yourself, "I can't do that"? What if instead you said to yourself, "I believe I can do it"?

Write about a time you felt confident or a time when you believed in yourself. What did you do? How did it feel?

_____

_____

_____

_____

_____

_____

_____

_____

_____

_____

Who do you believe you can be?

_____

_____

_____

_____

_____

_____

_____

_____

_____

_____

I can REACH my GOALS.

> "The work of today is the history of tomorrow, and we are its makers."
>
> Juliette Gordon Low

Goals give students something to work toward and a reason to work hard. In this unit, students will learn how to set goals and move toward achieving them.

★ Reading Passage: Juliette Gordon Low

The founder of the Girl Scouts had a singular vision: to unite and empower girls and make the world a better place.

★ Short-Answer Activity: Go for the Goal!

Students will reflect on the story of Juliette Gordon Low and the importance of creating goals. Students will share their answers with partners.

★ Small-Group Activity: Three Stars & One Wish

Students will gather in small groups and discover where they are already thriving and where they would like to improve.

★ Whole-Class Activity: SMART Goals

Together, the class will learn what it means to create meaningful, achievable goals. Students will have individual worksheets to complete, but will share and support one another's goals.

★ Journal Prompt: Ladder to Success

Students will reflect on how setting goals can help get them closer to their dreams.

★ Growing Beyond

To help students envision their future goals, they will create a vision board based on the goals they have defined.

Give each student a large piece of posterboard or construction paper. Provide cutout pictures from magazines, illustrations, and phrases that might be helpful as they create a future vision. Encourage students to dream big, and allow their creations to facilitate discussion about how they will achieve their dreams.

Name: _____   Date: _____

JULIETTE GORDON LOW

Juliette Gordon Low founded the Girl Scouts in 1912. Today, Girl Scouts everywhere know her story. But once, she was just a girl, too.

Juliette was born in Savannah, Georgia, in 1860. Her friends and family called her "Daisy." In school, Juliette loved music and art classes, athletics, animals, and nature. She also enjoyed spending time with her friends.

When Juliette was young, she injured her ear. She lost her hearing almost completely. But she didn't let that stop her from going after her dreams! She worked hard in school and loved to ride horses, hike, and play tennis. She studied painting in New York, too.

After she was married and moved to England, Juliette met Sir Robert Baden-Powell. He started the Boy Scouts. Juliette loved the idea. She helped start the Girl Guides (later called the Girl Scouts) in England.

Soon after, she moved back to Georgia. Now she had a new goal—to create a group for girls in the United States, too.

She called her cousin and said, "I've got something for the girls of Savannah, and all of America, and all the world, and we're going to start it tonight!"

Juliette started small. She gathered 18 girls together for the first troop of Girl Scouts. The girls learned how to cook, read a map, and apply first aid. When they mastered a new skill, they earned a badge.

The Girl Scouts became a national organization with troops all over the United States. Juliette wanted girls everywhere to believe in themselves and to grow and learn together. She never gave up on her vision.

Juliette achieved her goal. Today, there are more than three million members of the Girl Scouts all over the world!

Name: _____   **Date:** _____

· · · · · · GO FOR THE GOAL! · · · · · · ·

Directions: When Juliette Gordon Low returned from England, she was inspired to create the Girl Scouts in the United States. It became her *goal*.

It took time and effort for Juliette to achieve her goals, and it wasn't easy. Think about Juliette's story as you answer the questions below. Then share your answers with a partner.

1. As you read, Juliette had almost no hearing. Do you think that made it challenging at times to reach her goals? Why or why not?

   _____

   _____

   _____

2. Why do you think Juliette thought it was so important to create the Girl Scouts?

   _____

   _____

   _____

3. Have you ever made a goal for yourself? What was it? Did you achieve it?

   _____

   _____

   _____

4. Juliette was a strong leader. What qualities do you think make a good leader?

   _____

   _____

   _____

5. Sometimes, one person's goals can create a ripple effect that inspires others to set their own goals, too. What is one thing you could do that might inspire other people to set their goals?

   _____

   _____

   _____

Name: _____   **Date:** _____

THREE STARS & ONE WISH

Directions: Form a group with two to three other students. On your own, think of three things you do well. They can be any skill or quality you are proud of. Write each one inside a star. Then think of one thing you would wish for. Let it be something that is a challenge for you right now. Write it in the box at the bottom. When you're done, share what you wrote with your group.

My Wish

Name: _____   **Date:** _____

· · · · · · · · · · · · · SMART GOALS · · · · · · · · · ·

Directions: SMART goals are goals that we can track, work toward, and achieve. Create a goal for yourself, and then get together as a class and discuss what you will do to achieve your goal, and who can help you meet it. Add your notes below.

⭐ **S**pecific: What exactly do you want to do?

⭐ **M**easurable: How will you know if you did it?

⭐ **A**ttainable: Can you do it?

⭐ **R**elevant: Why is it important to you?

⭐ **T**imely: When will you have it done?

My Goal

I will _____

_____

_____

_____

_____

My Plan

The steps I will take to achieve my goal:

⭐ _____

⭐ _____

⭐ _____

Who can help me achieve my goal:

⭐ _____

⭐ _____

⭐ _____

Name: _____ **Date:** _____

LADDER TO SUCCESS

Now that you have a goal for your future, think about why it matters to you. Think about these questions, and write your answers on the lines below.

★ Why is your goal important to you?

★ How will you keep track of your goal? How often will you check back on it?

★ Who else will benefit from you achieving your goal?

★ How will you feel when you achieve your goal?

_____

_____

_____

_____

_____

_____

_____

_____

_____

_____

_____

_____

_____

_____

_____

_____

_____

_____

_____

_____

I am NOT afraid of DIFFICULT TASKS.

> "You can't set limits on what you can do."
>
> Shaquem Griffin

Facing difficulties is always challenging, but, in this unit, students can learn to face hardships with courage and perseverance on their journey to success.

★ Reading Passage: Shaquem Griffin

Some people told Shaquem Griffin that becoming a professional football player with just one hand was impossible, but he didn't let that stop him.

★ Short-Answer Activity: Determined to Succeed

With inspiration from the reading passage on Shaquem Griffin, students will reflect on facing difficulties with courage.

★ Small-Group Activity: How Hard Is This?

Students will rate and describe their reactions to imaginary situations in which difficulties are faced. Then they will compare their answers in small groups.

★ Whole-Class Activity: Keep Together

Students will make individual pledges on how they will face hard tasks. Then they will band together as a class to create class pledges to help one another when difficulties arise.

★ Journal Prompt: It's up to Me

Reflecting on a quote from Shaquem Griffin, students will write a letter to their future selves for the next time they want to give up.

★ Growing Beyond

As a class, watch the viral video "I Am Shaquem Griffin." Students will get to see Shaquem talk about the hardships he has faced and his determination to persevere.

After the viewing, discuss the concept of being "undefeated" as it is presented in the video and the idea of not giving up when things are hard.

Look up the word *perseverance* and ask students to think of someone else who has persevered in the face of difficulty.

Name: _____ Date: _____

SHAQUEM GRIFFIN

Shaquem Griffin doesn't let other people define him. He plays football for the NFL, but many people said he could never do that. He just didn't listen.

Shaquem was born with a condition that kept his left hand from fully developing. It was very painful, and he lost what he had of his hand.

But that never stopped him from going for what he wanted—to play football.

Others did not believe he could do it. They wondered how someone with one hand could play football.

Shaquem wasn't going to let others' doubts get in his way. As he said, "You can't set limits on what you can do, whether you have two hands or thirty hands. Show me what you can do, and we'll go from there."

To be a professional football player, he had to train hard and never give up. Shaquem wasn't afraid to face the difficult tasks ahead of him.

"When I started lifting weights, I remember I could barely bench the bar. I mean, I'm shaking all over the place, the bar's falling…but it just goes to show how much work I put in."

He decided to prove everyone wrong. "No matter if you have one hand or two hands, when someone tells you that you can't do something, the only thing you can do is just prove them wrong, no matter how hard it is."

With hard work and continued effort, Shaquem got stronger. He started breaking records. And the coaches and scouts who had doubted him were forced to give him a second look.

Shaquem is still setting records and working hard as a linebacker.

Name: _____   **Date:** _____

· · · · · · · · · DETERMINED TO SUCCEED · · · · · · · ·

Directions: Working with a partner, discuss each of these questions together. On your own, write your answers below.

1. What did you learn from reading about Shaquem? What is one thing you will take away from his story?

   _____

   _____

   _____

2. Shaquem Griffin didn't listen to people who doubted he could achieve his goals. How do you think he felt when others told him he couldn't do what he wanted to do? Why do you think he felt that way?

   _____

   _____

   _____

3. Do you think the fact that Shaquem only has one hand made him work harder for his goal? Why or why not?

   _____

   _____

   _____

4. What is one quality you admire in Shaquem? What do you have in common with him?

   _____

   _____

   _____

5. If you could ask Shaquem anything, what would you want to know?

   _____

   _____

   _____

Name: _____   **Date:** _____

· · · · · · · · · · · HOW HARD IS THIS? · · · · · · · · · · ·

Directions: On your own, read through these scenarios and think about how you would react. Rate and circle your reaction, and then describe what you would do.

Use this scale to rate your reaction:

1	**2**	**3**
I'm fine.	I'm a little bothered.	I'm upset.

When you're done, form a group with two to three other students. Choose one scenario you would like to share with the group, and discuss your answer.

1. There is a hard problem on a quiz, and you don't know how to get the answer.

   Rating: 1   2   3

   How I would handle this: _____

   _____

   _____

2. A teacher asks you to share your work, but you don't think you did the work right.

   Rating: 1   2   3

   How I would handle this: _____

   _____

   _____

3. A friend doesn't want to sit with you at lunchtime.

   Rating: 1   2   3

   How I would handle this: _____

   _____

   _____

4. You are asked to play a new game that you have never tried before.

   Rating: 1   2   3

   How I would handle this: _____

   _____

   _____

Name: _____   **Date:** _____

KEEP TOGETHER

Directions: When things get hard, it helps to have support from those around you. As a class, you can help one another by promising to be supportive when difficulties arise.

First, complete the statement below on your own. Share it with your classmates. Then write your class pledges here and save them so that you can look back and remember them when things get hard. See the example answers at the bottom of the page, or come up with your own answers.

When something gets difficult, I will _____

_____

_____

_____

_____

Our Class Pledges

When things get hard, we pledge to…

_____

_____

_____

When things get hard, we pledge to…

_____

_____

_____

When things get hard, we pledge to…

_____

_____

_____

When things get hard, we pledge to…

_____

_____

_____

- ★ help one another
- ★ ask for help
- ★ not give up
- ★ ask questions
- ★ try again
- ★ say "I can," not "I can't"
- ★ encourage one another
- ★ keep an open mind
- ★ stay positive

Name: _____ **Date:** _____

· · · · · · · · · · · · · · · · · IT'S UP TO ME · · · · · · · · · · · · · ·

"Don't set limits for me, because when I wake up in the morning and I brush my teeth and I look at myself in the mirror, it's only me that I see in the mirror. I'm not going to see anybody else in the mirror. That's how I live, day by day. When I look in the mirror, it's up to me to accomplish everything I want out of life."
—Shaquem Griffin

Difficult tasks are part of life. They come up all the time! What will you do the next time things get hard?

Write a letter to yourself for the next time you want to give up. What will you say to your future self to inspire you to keep going when things are difficult?

_____

_____

_____

_____

_____

_____

_____

_____

_____

_____

_____

_____

_____

_____

_____

_____

_____

_____

_____

_____

I can COME ★ UP with CREATIVE SOLUTIONS.

> "I dream for a living."
>
> Steven Spielberg

When obstacles get in the way, it can be challenging to keep going. Teaching students to come up with creative ways to solve problems is a perspective shift that will have lasting effects.

★ Reading Passage: Steven Spielberg

This legendary film director and producer has a gift for creativity, but even he has faced hardships that forced him to think outside of the box.

★ Short-Answer Activity: Overcoming Obstacles

Thinking about the reading passage on Steven Spielberg, students will reflect on approaching obstacles from different perspectives and gathering support. Then they will share their answers with partners.

★ Small-Group Activity: Save Fred

Working together in small groups, students will have to get creative to save Fred the gummy worm. Afterward, lead the class in a discussion of their solutions to the problem, highlighting those who were extra creative.

★ Whole-Class Activity: Acting Out

Students will use their creative problem-solving skills in a game of charades. Quietly tell each student the number of a situation they will act out. After the game, discuss as a class how students got creative with their pantomimes.

★ Journal Prompt: A Bigger Boat

Reflecting on what they have learned, students will write about how they look for solutions when things don't go as planned.

★ Growing Beyond

As a class, read *The Dot* by Peter H. Reynolds. Discuss as a class how the main character's teacher offers a new way to look at creativity, and how, through practice, the student inspires others to be creative, too.

Give each student a blank piece of paper with a simple black line, squiggle, or dot on it. Ask them what they see. Then have them create their own pictures from what they were given.

STEVEN SPIELBERG

Steven Spielberg has made some of the most creative movies audiences have ever seen— from *E.T.* and *Indiana Jones* to *Jurassic Park* and *The BFG*.

Steven always wanted to make movies. As a child, he borrowed his family's video camera to record family holidays and camping trips. When he was 12 years old, he made his first real movie.

He was only 16 when he made a movie about aliens. It was more than two hours long, and he made it in one night. His father rented out a local movie theater to show the film to a crowd.

Steven knew that making movies was the only thing he wanted to do. He wanted to go to film school, but his grades were not good enough for him to get into his dream college.

He had to get creative to follow his dreams. He went to a different college. Whenever he could, he went to the movies to study his craft. He spent time around the movie studios in Los Angeles, trying to learn as much as he could.

Soon, he made his first short film. Then he signed his first film contract. Steven was finally a professional director!

He had so many ideas he couldn't wait to share. But it wasn't always easy to make them into movies. When working on another alien movie, Steven felt stuck. He took a drive to clear his mind. That wasn't enough, so he stepped out and got on top of his car. He did a headstand. That was it! Seeing the Hollywood sign upside down, he had a vision. This was how the alien spaceship would look!

Steven's ability to get creative when things got hard helped him reach his dreams. He is now one of the most successful film directors in the world.

Name: _____ Date: _____

• • • • • • • OVERCOMING OBSTACLES • • • • • • • •

Directions: Think about what you read about Steven Spielberg. Then write your answers to the questions below. When you're done, share your answers with a partner.

1. In the reading passage, Steven stood on his head when he felt stuck. What are some other things he could have done to clear his mind? What do you do when you need to clear your mind?

   _____

   _____

   _____

   _____

2. Steven was surely disappointed that his grades weren't high enough to get into his dream film school. Do you think it would have been easy for Steven to give up on his dream at that point? What do you think made him decide to keep working toward becoming a director?

   _____

   _____

   _____

   _____

3. From a young age, Steven was interested in making movies. What is one thing you are interested in that you might like to study more? Why do you like doing it?

   _____

   _____

   _____

   _____

4. Steven's father supported his dream by renting out a local theater to show his son's first big movie. Is there someone you know that supports your dreams? How do they support you?

   _____

   _____

   _____

   _____

Name: _____   Date: _____

SAVE FRED

Directions: Fred needs your help! Work as a team with your three- or four-person group to find a way to save Fred from drowning. You may need to find some creative solutions to get the job done!

First, gather the items below for the game. Next, place the life preserver on the table. Third, turn the boat upside down and place it over the preserver. Finally, place Fred on top of the boat.

Items Needed

★ Fred (gummy worm)

★ Fred's life preserver (gummy ring)

★ Fred's boat (plastic cup)

★ 3–4 paper clips

Working together as a team, try to do the following:

1. Get Fred's boat right side up.

2. Put Fred back in his boat.

3. Place the life preserver on Fred.

Here are the rules:

1. You may only touch the paper clips! No one may touch the life preserver, the boat, or Fred with their hands.

2. You may not injure Fred.

Name: _____   **Date:** _____

ACTING OUT

Have you ever played charades? It's a riddle game in which you act out a phrase you are given while your friends guess what you're doing. The trick is that you have to stay silent! This means that you'll need your creativity to act out what you are trying to say.

Directions:

⭐ Read the situations listed below. Your teacher will quietly tell you the number of a situation you will act out.

⭐ Think of how you can act out this phrase without speaking a word.

⭐ When it's your turn, you will be called on to act out your situation. You may have to get creative to get your classmates to guess the right answer!

1. Running a race
2. Eating a pizza
3. Making a movie
4. Doing your homework
5. Surfing a wave
6. Shoveling snow
7. Having a picnic
8. Falling off a bicycle
9. Shopping for groceries
10. Drinking hot chocolate
11. Building a snowman
12. Singing an opera

13. Visiting the zoo
14. Baking cookies
15. Driving a school bus
16. Acting like a dog
17. Flying a kite
18. Jumping into a pile of leaves
19. Dancing in a ballet
20. Escaping from a bear
21. Taking out the trash
22. Celebrating your birthday
23. Riding a horse
24. Painting a portrait

Name: _____   **Date:** _____

· · · · · · · · · · · · A BIGGER BOAT · · · · · · · · · · ·

One of Steven Spielberg's most famous films, *Jaws*, is about the biggest shark anyone has ever seen. There is a famous quote from one of the characters, who says this after seeing the shark for the first time: "We're going to need a bigger boat." In other words, instead of giving up, we've got to find a better way. A new idea is a bigger boat!

Thinking back on what you have learned about finding creative solutions, write about your answers to these questions below.

★ When problems arise, how do you react? Do you get frustrated easily, or do you pause and ask yourself, "What is another way I could tackle this?"

★ If there is an obstacle in your way, how do you figure out how to get around it?

_____

_____

_____

_____

_____

_____

_____

_____

_____

_____

_____

_____

_____

_____

_____

_____

_____

_____

_____

I can IMPROVE with PRACTICE.

> "You have to fight to reach your dream. You have to sacrifice and work hard for it."
>
> ⚡ Lionel Messi

Practice doesn't make perfect—but it does make progress toward the goals we want to achieve. Through an inspiring story of dedication, students will discover that consistent practice can mean consistent improvement.

★ Reading Passage: Lionel Messi

International soccer superstar Lionel Messi was once thought to be too small to play soccer, but his determination to succeed made his dreams come true.

★ Short-Answer Activity: Determined to Improve

Using what they have learned from reading about Lionel Messi, students will answer questions about sacrifice and determination.

★ Small-Group Activity: Three-Part Stories

To practice active listening, students will create their own group stories. Place students into groups of three, and ask them each to contribute a sentence for a story (you choose the subject). Mix up the groups and ask them to repeat the story their group just created. Then have students record their stories.

★ Whole-Class Activity: Balloon Soccer

Students will practice working cooperatively with one another in a game of balloon soccer. Have students form a large circle and hold hands; keep a count of how many seconds they can keep the balloon air-bound without using their feet. They will discover that they must move together as a circle to keep it going! Add more balloons to add difficulty.

★ Journal Prompt: Better & Better

Students will reflect on one thing they have improved since a year ago, and what steps they have taken to achieve that improvement.

★ Growing Beyond

As a class, identify one skill or objective that the class needs to work on. Then create a progress chart together that will be a visible reminder of the goal. Consider offering a reward to the class when progress is made.

Name: _____ **Date:** _____

LIONEL MESSI

When soccer player Lionel Messi was a boy, no one thought he would someday be an international star.

Lionel grew up in Argentina. He started playing soccer when he was just four years old. He had watched his two older brothers play, and he fell in love with soccer too.

With his dad as his coach, Lionel practiced every day. Sometimes, he even missed playing with his friends so he could train instead. He dreamed of becoming a professional soccer player.

But when he was 11 years old, his parents noticed that he wasn't growing as fast as he should. They took him to a doctor and were given bad news. Lionel was missing a hormone he needed in order to grow properly.

Lionel's family did not have enough money for his treatment. They didn't know what they were going to do.

Through it all, Lionel never stopped training. He practiced hard, every day, to improve his skills.

By the time he was 13, a soccer team in Spain had heard of his talent. They offered him a spot on the team, and to pay for his treatment, too. He went for it.

Even though he was a little shorter than the other players, his hard work and practice paid off. Lionel started to break records and went on to become one of the most famous soccer players in history.

Working hard was the key to his success. He said, "I start early and I stay late, day after day, year after year. It took me 17 years and 114 days to become an overnight success."

Name: _____   **Date:** _____

· · · · · · · · · · DETERMINED TO IMPROVE · · · · · · · · · ·

Directions: In a group with two to three other students, take turns reading aloud each question below. Spend a few minutes individually writing your answers on the lines, and then discuss what you wrote with your group.

1. What was Lionel Messi's dream? Did he achieve it?

   _____

   _____

   _____

2. How do you think Lionel felt when he found out he wasn't growing properly? Do you think that made him work harder for his dream?

   _____

   _____

   _____

3. Look up the word *sacrifice*. What does it mean? What is a sacrifice that Lionel made for his dream?

   _____

   _____

   _____

4. It would have been easy for Lionel to give up on soccer when he was told he was too small to play. Why do you think he didn't give up?

   _____

   _____

   _____

5. Does Lionel's story inspire you? What is one thing you will remember about his story?

   _____

   _____

   _____

Name: _____   **Date:** _____

· · · · · · · · · · THREE-PART STORIES · · · · · · · · · ·

The first time you play a video game, you probably don't know how to win it. You have to keep practicing to get to the next level.

The same is true for any skill you want to achieve, whether it's becoming a professional soccer player, learning how to create slime, or becoming a better listener. The more you practice, the more progress you make!

Directions: Make up a story with two other students. Each person gets to offer one sentence. Your teacher will give you the subject for the story.

For example, maybe your subject is a pirate story. Student One says, "Captain Mateo had a parrot." Student Two adds, "The parrot spoke three languages." Student Three ends by saying, "Captain Mateo's parrot liked to read him bedtime stories."

Once each person has said their part of the story, repeat it back to one another. Then join a new group. Each person will take a turn telling their group's story to their new group. Practice listening closely so you can retell your story well! When you're done, write your group's story on the lines below.

_____

_____

_____

_____

_____

_____

_____

_____

_____

_____

_____

_____

_____

_____

Name: _____ **Date:** _____

• • • • • • • • • • • • BALLOON SOCCER • • • • • • • • • • • •

Directions: Get into a large circle and hold hands with your classmates. Your teacher will drop a balloon into the center of the circle. Your goal is to see how many times you can tap the balloon into the air and keep it moving, without losing your connection to the other students. The trick is, unlike a regular soccer game, you can't use your feet!

Here are the rules:

★ You can use your hands, arms, shoulders, knees, or head.

★ You cannot use your feet!

★ Try not to let go of your neighbor's hand.

★ If the balloon touches the ground or someone uses a foot, start over.

It might be challenging at first, but keep practicing! When the game is over, take a few moments on your own to write down what you thought of the game. What did you learn? Did the game get easier with more practice?

_____

_____

_____

_____

_____

_____

_____

_____

_____

_____

_____

_____

_____

_____

_____

Name: _____   **Date:** _____

· · · · · · · · · · · BETTER & BETTER · · · · · · · · · · ·

Lionel Messi said, "My ambition is always to get better and better."

Think back to this same time last year. Can you think of something that you have gotten better at since then?

What was it like back then? How did you feel? How have you improved since then? Did practice have anything to do with your improvement?

_____

_____

_____

_____

_____

_____

_____

_____

_____

_____

_____

_____

_____

_____

_____

_____

_____

_____

_____

★ I ★ value THOUGHTFUL FEEDBACK.

> "Even though an award was not meant to be, it's been heartwarming to hear from individuals who thought [*Starry River of the Sky*] was worthy. If anything it reminds me that my pact as an author is with the reader. I promise to create my absolute best for the readers of my books."
>
> Grace Lin

The ability to receive and implement feedback is a valuable skill in the growth mindset. In this unit, students will learn how to give and receive valuable feedback.

★ Reading Passage: Grace Lin

Author and illustrator Grace Lin loved making children's books, but she wasn't sure she was on the right path until she received some feedback that renewed her dedication to her craft.

★ Short-Answer Activity: Giving Feedback

Students will learn what feedback is and why we give it, reflecting on Grace Lin's story and their own experiences.

★ Small-Group Activity: Pair & Share

To practice giving valuable feedback, students will pair up and give each other feedback on a drawing they will create based on the title of one of Grace Lin's books. *Note:* Students will not need to read the book first to complete the activity. They should let their imaginations run wild!

★ Whole-Class Activity: Improve Your Story

Students are asked to write a story about their family, culture, or traditions and share it with the class for feedback. Ensure that all students have a chance to both give and receive feedback, and encourage them to make edits to their stories based on the feedback they receive.

★ Journal Prompt: Closing the Loop

Reflecting on how it felt to give and receive feedback will help students understand how valuable honest feedback can be.

★ Growing Beyond

Create a poster as a class that shows the difference between criticism and feedback, and examples of what each sounds like. Come up with a class rubric for how the group will give and receive feedback, and display it in the class so it can be easily referred to.

Name: _____   Date: _____

GRACE LIN

Grace Lin is an award-winning author and illustrator. Her books include *Where the Mountain Meets the Moon, Ling & Ting,* and *A Big Mooncake for Little Star.*

When Grace was young, she had dreams of becoming an ice skater. She used to draw pictures of herself twirling around on the ice. Those pictures inspired another dream: to write children's books.

Grace went to art school and soon created her first book, *The Ugly Vegetables.* Readers and critics loved her book, and she wanted to make another one.

But Grace felt stuck. She knew there was a story to tell, but it just wasn't coming out the way she wanted. She tried for three or four years to make the perfect book.

Then one day, she decided to stop trying to make her book something it didn't want to be. She kept writing, and that book became her first novel, *The Year of the Dog.*

At a book signing, a girl came up to Grace and told her how much she loved her books. She showed her a picture from when she was tiny, holding *The Ugly Vegetables.* Now this girl was reading *The Year of the Dog.* She was growing up reading Grace's books and loving them all.

Grace was so inspired! The girl's feedback made her realize that she was making a difference in readers' lives. She was motivated to make even more books!

Grace kept writing and drawing, and soon she had made more than a dozen books. Her books are different from many others because they are about her family and her Asian culture.

Name: _____   **Date:** _____

· · · · · · · · · · · GIVING FEEDBACK · · · · · · · · · · ·

What is feedback?

When you give feedback to someone, you are telling them what you think. You may be giving a suggestion or piece of advice for how they can improve their work.

Why do we give feedback?

Feedback helps us to improve. Sometimes, others see something in our work that we missed, or they have an idea that will make it even better.

In Grace Lin's story, the feedback she received from readers helped remind her why she was writing her books. The feedback inspired her to write even more stories.

Directions: Think about Grace Lin's story and your own experiences. Then answer the questions below.

1. Can you think of a time when you received feedback? Did it help you improve? How?

   _____

   _____

   _____

2. How do you feel when someone gives you feedback on your work? Why do you feel this way?

   _____

   _____

   _____

3. Have you ever given someone else feedback? How did they react?

   _____

   _____

   _____

4. How do you think Grace Lin felt when she received the feedback from the girl who read her books?

   _____

   _____

   _____

Name: _____   Date: _____

· · · · · · · · · · · · · · · · · · PAIR & SHARE · · · · · · · · · · · · · · · ·

Pair up to practice giving each other feedback. Remember, when you give feedback, you are clear, kind, and helpful.

Here are some ways to give feedback:

★ Give a compliment.   ★ Ask a question.   ★ Make a suggestion.

Directions: On your own, draw a picture that answers the question in the box below. Then find a partner. Bring your art with you, and sit together. Decide who will share first. The first person will share their picture and talk about what it means. The second person will give feedback and then share their artwork so the first person can give feedback, too.

What happens where the mountain meets the moon?

Name: _____   **Date:** _____

· · · · · · · · · IMPROVE YOUR STORY · · · · · · · · ·

Grace Lin's stories are based on her culture and her family's traditions.

For this exercise, you are going to write your own story about your family, culture, or traditions and share it with the class. You will receive feedback from your classmates to help make your story even better. You will also give valuable feedback to your classmates to help improve their stories.

Directions: On a separate piece of paper, write a story about your family, a tradition in your family, or something you love about your culture.

When everyone is done, you will be asked to share your story. You will need to listen carefully as you are receiving feedback about your work. Then you will need to listen to others tell their stories so you can give them feedback, too.

When you are receiving feedback, remember to:

⭐ Listen, not argue.

⭐ Think about the feedback you've received.

⭐ Thank the person for their feedback.

⭐ Decide on your own if you would like to make any changes to your story based on the feedback you received.

When you are giving feedback, remember to:

⭐ Be clear, kind, and helpful.

⭐ State something you liked first.

⭐ Ask a question or give advice.

Write down the most valuable piece of feedback you received here:

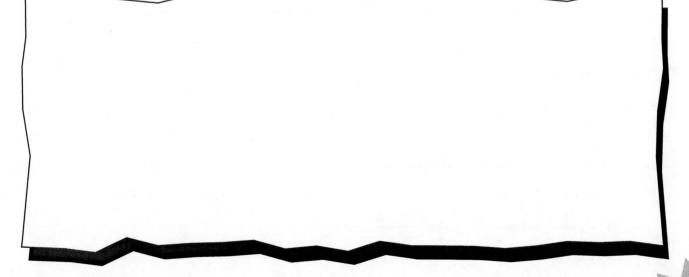

Name: _____   **Date:** _____

CLOSING THE LOOP

Bill Gates said, "We all need people who will give us feedback. That's how we improve."

How did it feel to receive feedback from your classmates? Did any of the feedback you received help make your story better? Write about what you learned about feedback and how it will help you in the future.

_____

_____

_____

_____

_____

_____

_____

_____

_____

_____

_____

_____

_____

_____

_____

_____

_____

_____

_____

_____

I am CAPABLE of learning NEW THINGS.

> "Don't allow someone else to decide what you are capable of—
> you decide what you want to accomplish."
>
> Amberley Snyder

Learning something new isn't always easy. Teaching students the "power of yet" and helping them discover they can learn new things, even when it gets hard, will provide a solid foundation for growth.

★ Reading Passage: Amberley Snyder

When rodeo racer Amberley Snyder was just 18, she lost the use of her legs in a horrible accident. Relearning everything from a wheelchair, she never stopped working toward her dreams.

★ Short-Answer Activity: Motivated to Move

Reflecting on the reading passage, students will explore the definition of *motivation* and how it feels to have to work hard to reach your goals. Then they will answer comprehension questions and share their answers with a partner.

★ Small-Group Activity: The Power of Yet

In pairs, students will create a list of things they can do and things they can't do YET. Then they will share their lists with each other.

★ Whole-Class Activity: Not Yet, But Soon!

Building off the small-group activity, students will use a graphic organizer to define what they will do to learn one thing in their "not yet" list. Ask students to share their ideas with the class, and create a bulletin board to display the students' work so it can remain a focal point.

★ Journal Prompt: Keep Learning

Students will reflect on what motivates them to keep learning and what it means to work hard at continued learning.

★ Growing Beyond

Define a class goal that everyone can work toward together. It could be a learning goal, a charitable donation, or anything measurable. The idea is to help students have a tangible goal for the future that they have not reached YET, but through their efforts together and in small steps, can make a reality.

Name: _____   Date: _____

AMBERLEY SNYDER

Amberley Snyder started riding horses when she was three years old. At seven, she was already riding in the rodeo. In high school, she became a rodeo champion.

But when she was 18, she was in a terrible car accident. She wasn't wearing a seatbelt, and she lost the use of her legs.

Doctors told her she would never walk again. But she had a goal for herself. Not only did she want to walk, but she wanted to ride a horse again and compete in the rodeo.

Working toward her new goal wasn't easy. Amberley had to learn how to do everything all over again. She had to learn how to put her horse's saddle on. She had to learn how to take care of her horse from her wheelchair.

There were a lot of hard days. But Amberley was determined to reach her goals. She wasn't afraid of learning new things.

"It was definitely an adjustment, and I had to adjust my goals," Amberley said. She worked hard, and soon, she learned how to get back in the saddle again.

She even fitted her saddle with a new seatbelt. Soon, she was racing again! Amberley and her horse, Power, started racing faster than they did before the accident.

Amberley now makes videos about everything she has learned to do since her accident. She posts "Wheelchair Wednesday" videos that show how she does things from her wheelchair. She wrote a book called *Walk. Ride. Rodeo.* that was made into a movie about her life.

Today, she still has a goal: to walk again. Amberley is still learning, and she is not giving up on her goal.

Name: _____ **Date:** _____

MOTIVATED TO MOVE

Directions: Think about Amberley's story. Then write your answers to the questions below. Find a partner and share your answers.

1. After her accident, Amberley was determined to get back on her horse, even though she couldn't even walk yet. How do you think she felt when her doctors said she wouldn't walk again?

   _____

   _____

   _____

2. Look up the word *motivation*. What do you think was Amberley's motivation to keep working toward her goal?

   _____

   _____

   _____

3. Imagine what it would be like to have to relearn how to do everything without the use of your legs. What is one thing you think would be challenging to relearn?

   _____

   _____

   _____

4. Why do you think Amberley never gave up on her dream of walking and riding again?

   _____

   _____

   _____

5. What is one question you would ask Amberley if you could?

   _____

   _____

   _____

Name: _____   Date: _____

THE POWER OF YET

When something is hard or new, we sometimes say to ourselves, "I can't do that." But there is one word we can add to that sentence that changes everything: YET. When we say, "I can't do that YET," we are allowing some space for us to learn how to do the thing we want to do.

Directions: Amberley Snyder had to relearn how to do almost everything without the use of her legs. Even if she couldn't do something at first, she believed she could do it someday. Thinking about Amberley's story, write down some things you can do and some things you can't do YET. Then find a partner and share your lists.

I am really good at...

_____

_____

_____

_____

_____

_____

I haven't learned how to _____ YET!

_____

_____

_____

_____

_____

Name: _____   Date: _____

NOT YET, BUT SOON!

Directions: Draw a self-portrait in the oval. Then think of one thing you haven't learned yet that you would like to work on, and write it on the line.

Now, think of three steps you could take to move you closer to meeting your "yet." Write them down.

Finally, draw a picture of what it will look like when you learn your "yet." If you need more room, use a separate piece of paper.

I can't _____ YET...

But if I...

List three things you can do to help you learn.

1. _____

2. _____

3. _____

I will!

Not yet, but soon!

Name: _____ **Date:** _____

· · · · · · · · · · KEEP LEARNING · · · · · · · · · ·

Amberley Snyder said, "My goals have not changed. I'm just giving myself a little more time to accomplish them."

Think back on something you've learned that was not easy at first. What were the steps you had to take to learn the new thing? How did it feel to learn something new? What was your motivation to keep learning?

_____

_____

_____

_____

_____

_____

_____

_____

_____

_____

_____

_____

_____

_____

_____

_____

_____

_____

_____

_____

_____

_____

I can KEEP GOING when THINGS are TOUGH.

> "We can push ourselves further. We always have more to give."
>
> **Simone Biles**

When the going gets tough, students may need to rely on grit to persevere and achieve their goals. In this unit, students will learn how being gritty can bring success.

⭐ **Reading Passage: Simone Biles**

World-champion gymnast Simone Biles overcame a challenging childhood to excel in her sport beyond all expectations.

⭐ **Short-Answer Activity: GRIT Is Good**

Students will learn what "grit" is, and how it can help with goal achievement and excellence. Then they will answer questions based on the narrative.

⭐ **Small-Group Activity: How Gritty Are You?**

In small groups, students will help one another define characteristics of *grit* and then describe a moment when they felt they showed grit.

⭐ **Whole-Class Activity: Gritty Heroes**

The class will create a list of admirable heroes who have shown grit. To prep the class for this activity, it may help to brainstorm familiar movie and book characters who are gritty. List the names and evidence students come up with on a whiteboard or poster.

⭐ **Journal Prompt: I've Got Grit**

Reflecting on what it takes to keep going when times are tough, students will write about their own grittiness.

⭐ **Growing Beyond**

Ask students to conduct grit interviews outside of the classroom. They should choose someone who is an adult, is not a relative, and has achieved a goal. After interviews are complete, challenge students to tell the story they learned creatively—through a presentation, an art project, or a 3-D model.

Name: _____   Date: _____

· · · · · · · · · SIMONE BILES · · · · · · · · ·

Olympic gold-medalist Simone Biles is a world champion. But her story didn't start out like a fairy tale.

Her mother and father couldn't take care of Simone and her siblings. It was a hard time, with Simone and her siblings moving in and out of foster care. When she was three, she was adopted by her grandparents.

When Simone was only six years old, her class took a field trip to a local gymnastics class. Simone was copying their moves, and one of the coaches noticed. They asked Simone's family if she could train, too.

Simone fell in love with gymnastics, and she started training hard. She knew that someday, she wanted to go to the Olympics.

Her grandmother would sit down with her every year to help Simone write a list of her goals for the year to come.

Simone has said, "Everyone around you can tell you, 'Oh, you can do this,' but whenever you really start to believe in yourself, that's when it comes to life. But you also have to be a little bit fearless."

Simone's hard work paid off, and she started winning competitions. Sometimes, it was tough to get going. Sometimes, she fell or didn't want to work anymore. But her coaches wouldn't let her quit. They motivated her to keep trying and do it again.

Simone had to give up a lot to train hard. When she is training to compete, she trains for six to eight hours a day!

Simone's pledge to always give her best has made her a champion. She has won more than 20 world medals. That is more than anyone in US history!

Name: _____   **Date:** _____

GRIT IS GOOD

Simone Biles went through tough times to become a world champion. Through it all, she never gave up, and she was passionate about her goals. You could call this GRIT.

⭐ **G**ive it your all.

⭐ **R**edo if necessary.

⭐ **I**gnore giving up.

⭐ **T**ake time to do it right.

People with GRIT never give up, even when things get tough.

Directions: Think about Simone's story. Then answer the questions below.

1. Simone once said, "A successful competition for me is always going out there and putting 100 percent into whatever I'm doing." What happens when you give 100 percent of your effort to a goal?

   _____

   _____

   _____

2. When she was on her way to becoming a gold-medalist, do you think Simone ever wanted to give up? Why or why not?

   _____

   _____

   _____

3. Would you say that Simone Biles has GRIT? Why do you think so?

   _____

   _____

   _____

4. Name someone else you think has GRIT. What is it about this person that makes you think they are gritty?

   _____

   _____

   _____

Name: _____   Date: _____

HOW GRITTY ARE YOU?

Directions: In a group with two to three other students, create a grit poster together.

1. On a large piece of paper or posterboard, brainstorm what *grit* means. Write this at the top of the page:

Grit is...

2. Leave some room at the bottom, where you will eventually be pasting your answers.

3. Talk about ways you have seen other people be gritty. Think of a time when *you* were gritty.

4. Fill out the box below with your grit story, and then cut it out and glue it to your group's grit poster.

I showed how gritty I am when...

Name: _____ **Date:** _____

· · · · · · · · · GRITTY HEROES · · · · · · · · · ·

Here is another way we can define *grit*.

- ★ **G** is for Goals.
- ★ **R** is for Resilience.
- ★ **I** is for Intention.
- ★ **T** is for Time.

Simone Biles had a goal of getting on the Olympic team. She showed resilience when she faced hardships and kept going. Simone had the intention of always giving her best effort. She put in the time and hard work to achieve her dreams.

Directions: As a class, make a list of gritty heroes. To begin, on your own, list one person you think of as a gritty hero. Write down one thing for each letter that shows how your hero is gritty. Then share your answers with the class.

Gritty Hero: _____

G _____

(What goal did my hero set?)

_____

R _____

(What resilience did my hero show?)

_____

I _____

(What intention did my hero have?)

_____

T _____

(What kind of time did my hero put in to learn?)

_____

Name: _____   **Date:** _____

• • • • • • • • • • • • • I'VE GOT GRIT • • • • • • • • • • • •

"If they said, 'Do five pull-ups,' I would always want to do ten."—Simone Biles

Simone Biles kept going, even when times were tough. She never lost sight of her dream of becoming an Olympic gymnast.

Write about a time when things were hard for you, but you were gritty and kept going. What did you think about? How did you feel? What made you keep going?

_____

_____

_____

_____

_____

_____

_____

_____

_____

_____

_____

_____

_____

_____

_____

_____

_____

_____

_____

_____

_____

_____

I can TRAIN MY BRAIN.

> "To paint is the most terrific thing that there is, but to do it well is very difficult."
>
> Frida Kahlo

Our brains change as we grow, and teaching students a growth mindset empowers them to feel that they can become proficient in anything they put their efforts toward.

★ Reading Passage: Frida Kahlo

After a horrific accident that left her bedridden, Frida Kahlo taught herself to paint and became one of the world's most inspiring artists.

★ Short-Answer Activity: Grow Your Brain

First individually, and then in pairs, students will reflect on the reading about Frida Kahlo and be introduced to the idea of our changing brains.

★ Small-Group Activity: Fixed or Growth?

Explain the idea of fixed vs. growth mindsets to the class, and then ask students to work together in small groups to place fixed- and growth-mindset statements in the right spots. Discuss as a class when complete.

★ Whole-Class Activity: Brain Training

On a whiteboard or posterboard, make two columns titled "What I Should Tell My Brain" and "What NOT to Tell My Brain." As a class, discuss growth and fixed mindsets and ask students to record their own version of the class discussion on the provided worksheet.

★ Journal Prompt: Imagine If...

Students are asked to imagine what they would train their brains to do, just like Frida Kahlo taught herself to paint.

★ Growing Beyond

Have students build a brain model out of clay or play dough. Discuss each part of the brain, what it does, and how we use it. Ask students to label the brains they create, and discuss the idea of brain plasticity in more detail so they understand how brains can change and grow, too.

Name: _____   Date: _____

FRIDA KAHLO

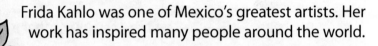

Frida Kahlo was one of Mexico's greatest artists. Her work has inspired many people around the world.

But she might never have become an artist if it hadn't been for an accident. When she was a teenager, she was riding a bus that crashed into a trolley.

She was hurt badly. She broke her back in three places and also broke her pelvis and collarbone. Frida had to wear a full body cast for three months to recover. She could barely move! As she lay there, she knew she needed to find something to do to pass the time and help her forget about her pain.

Frida decided to train her brain to do something new. She had always loved drawing, but that was too hard to do lying down.

Painting seemed like something good to try. Her parents gave her brushes and paints and everything she needed. They even made her a special easel she could use to paint in bed. They hung a mirror above her so she could see her reflection and paint pictures of herself.

Frida fell in love with painting. Mostly, she painted self-portraits. As she said, "I paint myself because I am often alone and I am the subject I know best."

It took time, but Frida slowly recovered from her injuries. She kept painting after she could finally get out of her bed.

She taught herself, and the more she painted, the more famous her work became. While her injuries caused her pain for the rest of her life, she always treasured her artwork. To this day, some of her most famous paintings are her self-portraits.

Name: _____   **Date:** _____

· · · · · · · · · · · GROW YOUR BRAIN · · · · · · · · · · ·

Directions: Answer the questions below, and then share your answers with a partner.

1. Frida Kahlo learned a new skill: how to paint. What is a new skill you have learned recently? What steps did you take to learn it?

    _____

    _____

2. Your brain is what helps you learn. And it's just like a muscle—the more you exercise your brain, the stronger it grows. What is one thing you could do today to exercise your brain?

    _____

    _____

3. Did you know that laughing can make your brain and memory stronger? Frida said, "Nothing is worth more than laughter. It is strength to laugh and…to be light." What makes you laugh?

    _____

    _____

4. In Frida's self-portraits, she didn't just paint herself in bed. She painted herself in all kinds of places from her imagination. Draw a picture of yourself in someplace from your imagination. If you need more room, use a separate piece of paper.

Name: _____ **Date:** _____

FIXED OR GROWTH?

Directions: Form a group with two to three other students. One student can cut out the statements at the bottom of this page. Another student can use their page for everyone to work on.

Place each statement where it belongs, either on the *Fixed Mindset* side or the *Growth Mindset* side. Be sure everyone agrees before you place each statement where it belongs. When you're done, discuss as a class what you discovered.

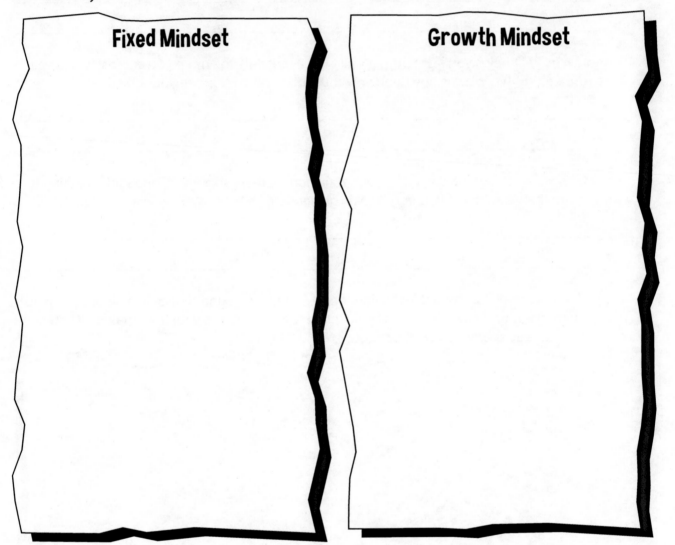

★ I can't do this.	★ I'm not good at this.	★ I can always improve.
★ This is too hard.	★ I can learn from my mistakes.	★ I will keep trying.
★ I will try to figure it out.	★ I will do my best.	★ I'll never get this right.
★ I don't know yet.	★ It's good enough.	★ I want to learn.

Name: _____   **Date:** _____

· · · · · · · · · · · BRAIN TRAINING · · · · · · · · · ·

Directions: As a class, discuss some thoughts you can say to your brain to help it grow. Take notes from your class discussion here so you can refer back to it later. At the bottom, there are some ideas for some statements you could add to the class discussion.

What I Should Tell My Brain	What NOT to Tell My Brain

⭐ People can change. ⭐ I'm just not that smart. ⭐ This subject isn't for me.

⭐ What strategy can I use? ⭐ I like a challenge. ⭐ Mistakes help me learn.

Name: _____ **Date:** _____

IMAGINE IF...

Imagine that you, like Frida, have to stay in your room for three months. What would you teach yourself how to do? Why? What are the steps you would take to teach yourself this skill? Write your answers on the lines below.

_____

_____

_____

_____

_____

_____

_____

_____

_____

_____

_____

_____

_____

_____

_____

_____

_____

_____

_____

_____

_____

_____

Most of the activities in *Change Your Mindset: Growth Mindset Activities for the Classroom* meet one or more of the following Common Core State Standards © Copyright 2010. National Governors Association Center for Best Practices and Council of Chief State School Officers. All rights reserved. For more information about the Common Core State Standards, go to *http://www.corestandards.org/* or *http://www.teachercreated.com/standards/*.

Grade 3	
Reading: Informational Text	**Activity Title (Unit #)**
Key Ideas and Details	
ELA.RI.3.1: Ask and answer questions to demonstrate understanding of a text, referring explicitly to the text as the basis for the answers.	Time & Effort (2), Beautiful Mistakes (3), Confidence Is Key (4), Go for the Goal! (5), Determined to Succeed (6), Overcoming Obstacles (7), Determined to Improve (8), Giving Feedback (9), Motivated to Move (10)
Range of Reading and Level of Text Complexity	
ELA.RI.3.10: By the end of the year, read and comprehend informational texts, including history/social studies, science, and technical texts, at the high end of the grades 2–3 text complexity band independently and proficiently.	Jesse Owens (1), Sidney Poitier (2), James Dyson (3), Oprah Winfrey (4), Juliette Gordon Low (5), Shaquem Griffin (6), Steven Spielberg (7), Lionel Messi (8), Grace Lin (9), Amberley Snyder (10), Simone Biles (11), Frida Kahlo (12)
Writing	**Activity Title (Unit #)**
Text Types and Purposes	
ELA.W.3.2: Write informative/explanatory texts to examine a topic and convey ideas and information clearly.	Invented by Mistake (3)
ELA.W.3.3: Write narratives to develop real or imagined experiences or events using effective technique, descriptive details, and clear event sequences.	Your Best (1), Believe It, Be It (4), Three-Part Stories (8), Improve Your Story (9), How Gritty Are You? (11), I've Got Grit (11), Imagine If… (12)
Production and Distribution of Writing	
ELA.W.3.4: With guidance and support from adults, produce writing in which the development and organization are appropriate to task and purpose.	Doing Your Best (1), The Best of Me (1), Your Best (1), Growing Beyond (1), Time & Effort (2), 10,000 Hours (2), Practice Makes Progress (2), Growing Beyond (2), Beautiful Mistakes (3), Invented by Mistake (3), The Most Magnificent Thing (3), Try, Try Again (3), Growing Beyond (3), Confidence Is Key (4), Say Something Nice (4), Expert Advice (4), Believe It, Be It (4), Growing Beyond (4), Go for the Goal! (5), Three Stars & One Wish (5), SMART Goals (5), Ladder to Success (5), Determined to Succeed (6), How Hard Is This? (6), Keep Together (6), It's Up to Me (6), Overcoming Obstacles (7), A Bigger Boat (7), Determined to Improve (8), Three-Part Stories (8), Better & Better (8), Giving Feedback (9), Improve Your Story (9), Closing the Loop (9), Growing Beyond (9), Motivated to Move (10), The Power of Yet (10), Not Yet, But Soon! (10), Keep Learning (10), GRIT Is Good (11), How Gritty Are You? (11), Gritty Heroes (11), I've Got Grit (11), Grow Your Brain (12), Imagine If… (12)
Speaking & Listening	**Activity Title (Unit #)**
Comprehension and Collaboration	
ELA.SL.3.1: Engage effectively in a range of collaborative discussions (one-on-one, in groups, and teacher-led) with diverse partners on *grade 3 topics and texts*, building on others' ideas and expressing their own clearly.	Doing Your Best (1), The Best of Me (1), Growing Beyond (1), Time & Effort (2), How Much Effort Do I Give? (2), Growing Beyond (2), Beautiful Mistakes (3), Confidence Is Key (4), Go for the Goal! (5), Three Stars & One Wish (5), SMART Goals (5), Determined to Succeed (6), How Hard Is This? (6), Growing Beyond (6), Overcoming Obstacles (7), Determined to Improve (8), Pair & Share (9), Improve Your Story (9), Motivated to Move (10), Gritty Heroes (11), Grow Your Brain (12), Fixed or Growth? (12), Brain Training (12)
Presentation of Knowledge and Ideas	
ELA.SL.3.4: Report on a topic or text, tell a story, or recount an experience with appropriate facts and relevant, descriptive details, speaking clearly at an understandable pace.	Time & Effort (2), Beautiful Mistakes (3), Expert Advice (4), Go for the Goal! (5), Growing Beyond (7), Determined to Improve (8), Improve Your Story (9)

Grade 4

Reading: Informational Text	Activity Title (Unit #)
Key Ideas and Details	
ELA.RI.4.1: Refer to details and examples in a text when explaining what the text says explicitly and when drawing inferences from the text.	Time & Effort (2), Beautiful Mistakes (3), Confidence Is Key (4), Go for the Goal! (5), Determined to Succeed (6), Overcoming Obstacles (7), Determined to Improve (8), Giving Feedback (9), Motivated to Move (10)
Range of Reading and Level of Text Complexity	
ELA.RI.4.10: By the end of year, read and comprehend informational texts, including history/social studies, science, and technical texts, in the grades 4–5 text complexity band proficiently, with scaffolding as needed at the high end of the range.	Jesse Owens (1), Sidney Poitier (2), James Dyson (3), Oprah Winfrey (4), Juliette Gordon Low (5), Shaquem Griffin (6), Steven Spielberg (7), Lionel Messi (8), Grace Lin (9), Amberley Snyder (10), Simone Biles (11), Frida Kahlo (12)

Writing	Activity Title (Unit #)
Text Types and Purposes	
ELA.W.4.2: Write informative/explanatory texts to examine a topic and convey ideas and information clearly.	Invented by Mistake (3)
ELA.W.4.3: Write narratives to develop real or imagined experiences or events using effective technique, descriptive details, and clear event sequences.	Your Best (1), Believe It, Be It (4), Three-Part Stories (8), Improve Your Story (9), How Gritty Are You? (11), I've Got Grit (11), Imagine If… (12)
Production and Distribution of Writing	
ELA.W.4.4: Produce clear and coherent writing in which the development and organization are appropriate to task, purpose, and audience.	Doing Your Best (1), The Best of Me (1), Your Best (1), Growing Beyond (1), Time & Effort (2), 10,000 Hours (2), Practice Makes Progress (2), Growing Beyond (2), Beautiful Mistakes (3), Invented by Mistake (3), The Most Magnificent Thing (3), Try, Try Again (3), Growing Beyond (3), Confidence Is Key (4), Say Something Nice (4), Expert Advice (4), Believe It, Be It (4), Growing Beyond (4), Go for the Goal! (5), Three Stars & One Wish (5), SMART Goals (5), Ladder to Success (5), Determined to Succeed (6), How Hard Is This? (6), Keep Together (6), It's Up to Me (6), Overcoming Obstacles (7), A Bigger Boat (7), Determined to Improve (8), Three-Part Stories (8), Better & Better (8), Giving Feedback (9), Improve Your Story (9), Closing the Loop (9), Growing Beyond (9), Motivated to Move (10), The Power of Yet (10), Not Yet, But Soon! (10), Keep Learning (10), GRIT Is Good (11), How Gritty Are You? (11), Gritty Heroes (11), I've Got Grit (11), Grow Your Brain (12), Imagine If… (12)

Speaking & Listening	Activity Title (Unit #)
Comprehension and Collaboration	
ELA.SL.4.1: Engage effectively in a range of collaborative discussions (one-on-one, in groups, and teacher-led) with diverse partners on *grade 4 topics and texts,* building on others' ideas and expressing their own clearly.	Doing Your Best (1), The Best of Me (1), Growing Beyond (1), Time & Effort (2), How Much Effort Do I Give? (2), Growing Beyond (2), Beautiful Mistakes (3), Confidence Is Key (4), Go for the Goal! (5), Three Stars & One Wish (5), SMART Goals (5), Determined to Succeed (6), How Hard Is This? (6), Growing Beyond (6), Overcoming Obstacles (7), Determined to Improve (8), Pair & Share (9), Improve Your Story (9), Motivated to Move (10), Gritty Heroes (11), Grow Your Brain (12), Fixed or Growth? (12), Brain Training (12)
Presentation of Knowledge and Ideas	
ELA.SL.4.4: Report on a topic or text, tell a story, or recount an experience in an organized manner, using appropriate facts and relevant, descriptive details to support main ideas or themes; speak clearly at an understandable pace.	Time & Effort (2), Beautiful Mistakes (3), Expert Advice (4), Go for the Goal! (5), Growing Beyond (7), Determined to Improve (8), Improve Your Story (9)

#8310 Change Your Mindset